History's Yearbook

GIRL SCIENTISTS

Virginia Loh-Hagan

But I was free, and they should be free.
-Harriet Tubman

I am not afraid... I was born to do this.
-Joan of Arc

It's the little things citizens do. That's what will make the difference. My little thing is planting trees.
-Victoria Woodhull

I am a queen. And as long as I live, I will reign.
-Zenobia

To create one's world in any of the arts takes courage.
-Georgia O'Keeffe

side of the room and the guys on the other side of the room. I guess they didn't want to associate with me. But I could hold my own with them and sometimes did better.
-Mary Golda Ross

A woman is like a tea bag. You can't tell how strong she is until you put her in hot water.
-Eleanor Roosevelt

The world has used me so unkindly...
...ary Anning

If you hold your hand closed, nothing good can come in. The open hand is ble- ... it gives in abundance, even as ...es.
-Biddy Mason

Liberty!
–Inayat Khan's last word

I've never been afraid in my life.
-Nancy Wake

I attribute my success to this: I never gave or took any excuse.
–Florence Nightingale

Women should be someone, and not something.
–Mary Cassatt

Well-behaved women seldom make history.
-Laurel Thatcher Ulrich

Here is the day. We must welcome it with song.
–Marie Laveau

The title of Queen rang sweet to my ears.
-Catherine the Great

Contents

Introduction

We are celebrating girl scientists! Scientists study many topics. They study space. They study plants. They study medicine. They study rocks. Science is everywhere!

Scientists work in **STEM** jobs. STEM stands for science, technology, engineering, and math. Women have had to overcome many challenges in these fields.

But it hasn't been easy being a girl scientist. Things have changed. There are many female scientists today. But what took so long?

Throughout history, women have shown that they're tough. They're smart. They're strong. The girl scientists in this book rise to the top. They paved the way for today's girl scientists. Working in STEM is more than just crunching numbers and figuring out formulas. It is about solving mysteries. It's about making something work. It's about dreaming and using your imagination. Do you like to solve, create, and imagine? Then you have the qualities of a scientist!

Here's to you and all the girl scientists in our lives!

chapter 1

BEST ALL-AROUND

Marie Curie

> Nothing in life is to be feared. It is only to be understood. Now is the time to understand more, so that we can fear less.
>
> –Marie Curie

The "Best All-Around" award goes to Marie Curie! Curie made important discoveries. She studied rays. She discovered two elements. Elements are substances in chemistry.

She helped develop x-ray machines that could travel. X-rays are special energy. They pass through things. X-ray machines take pictures inside bodies. At the time, these machines were only in big cities. World War I was happening. Soldiers needed to be x-rayed. But the battlefields were far from the city. Curie helped. She invented special x-ray machines. The machines moved. They traveled to hurt soldiers on battlefields.

Curie won 2 Nobel Prizes. She was the only woman to win twice. Her work saved many lives. She also inspired other women to study science.

chapter 2

MOST INSPIRIED

Chien-Shiung Wu

There is only one thing worse than coming home from the lab to a sink full of dirty dishes. And that is not going to the lab at all.

–Chien-Shiung Wu

The “Most Inspired” award goes to Chien-Shiung Wu. Wu was born in China. She read a book about Marie Curie. This inspired her to be a scientist like Curie. Wu has been called the “Chinese Madame Curie.”

She moved to the United States. In 1944, she joined the Manhattan Project. This was a top-secret project. This project made the first atomic bomb. Atomic bombs are weapons. They have great exploding power.

Wu was the only Chinese person to work in the war department. She was one of the only top women scientists on the Manhattan Project.

chapter 3

MOST LIKELY TO HAVE THE BEST GARDEN

Ynes Mexia

> She loved the wild ... she always wanted to do things differently from the way others did.
>
> –Nina Floy Bracelin (assistant to Ynes Mexia)

The "Most Likely to Have the Best Garden" award goes to Ynes Mexia. Mexia was Mexican American. She was a **botanist**. Botany is the study of plants. Mexia was the best plant collector of her time.

She went on many collecting trips. She collected over 150,000 plants. She discovered new plants. She traveled to many places. She traveled all over Mexico and South America. She started doing this at age 55. She fell off cliffs. She went up the Amazon River.

She lived in many places. She was born in Washington, D.C. She spent her childhood in Texas. She went to school in Maryland, Philadelphia, and Canada. She moved to Mexico City. She died in California. She died in 1938.

chapter 4

MOST PATRIOTIC

Ruby Sakae Hirose

> We were American citizens. We were incarcerated by our American government in American internment camps here in the United States.
>
> –George Takei (Japanese American actor)

The "Most **Patriotic**" award goes to Ruby Sakae Hirose. Patriotic means loyal to one's country. Hirose was Japanese American. She was a doctor. She was a scientist. She did a lot of research. Her work helped stop polio. Polio was a sickness. Hirose helped create a **vaccine**. Vaccines are medicine. They stop sicknesses from happening.

During World War II, the United States was fighting Japan. This affected Japanese Americans in the United States. They were treated unfairly. They were taken from their homes. They were sent to internment camps. Internment means jail. Hirose was working in Ohio. She was saved from internment. But her family was interned.

Hirose helped the United States. She helped even though the United States hurt her family. She wanted everyone to be healthy. She had a big heart.

chapter 5

MOST UNDERRATED PLAYER

Lise Meitner

> You must not blame us scientists for the use which war technicians have put our discoveries.
>
> –Lise Meitner

The "Most Underrated Player" award goes to Lise Meitner. Underrated means to rate too low. Meitner was Austrian. She was the first female **physics** professor in Germany. Physics is the study of matter and energy. Meitner was forced to leave her job. It was because she was Jewish.

Meitner's work was important. She discovered nuclear fission. Nuclear fission leads to a big explosion. It creates energy. It creates power.

The Nobel Prize was given to Meitner's partner. Her partner was a man. It wasn't fair. She wasn't given any credit. Credit is praise and recognition. Meitner died in 1968. She was given awards and honors after she died.

chapter 6

MOST DRIVEN

Susan La Flesche Picotte

> It has always been a desire of mine to study medicine ever since I was a small girl, for even then I saw the need of my people for a good physician.
>
> –Susan La Flesche Picotte

The "Most **Driven**" award goes to Susan La Flesche Picotte. Driven means very determined to succeed. Picotte watched a Native American die. A white doctor refused to treat her. This inspired Picotte. She became the first Native American doctor. She was a top student. She treated other Native Americans. In 1913, she helped build a hospital for her people.

She had many other talents. She spoke several languages. She spoke her Omaha Native American language. She spoke English. She spoke French. She learned to paint. She played the piano. She quoted the Bible. She quoted Shakespeare. Shakespeare was a famous writer.

Picotte learned to live in two worlds. But she never forgot her Native American culture.

chapter 7

MOST LIKELY TO AIM HIGH

Caroline Herschel

Still, as I cannot do much at a time, I wish yet to live a little longer. For it is with me, as I suppose it is with everybody, we always have something yet to do.

–Caroline Herschel

The "Most Likely to Aim High" award goes to Caroline Herschel. Herschel faced challenges. She was 4 feet and 3 inches (1.3 meters) tall. She was blind in her left eye. She was denied an education. She helped her brother with his **astronomy** work. Astronomy is the study of space.

She was the first woman to discover a new **comet**. Comets are bright objects in space. They have long tails. She discovered 8 comets total.

Herschel discovered new **nebulae**. Nebulae are space clouds. They're made of dust and gases. Herschel discovered over 550 new stars.

chapter 8

BEST COLLECTOR

Mary Anning

The world has used me so unkindly. I fear it has made me suspicious of everyone.

–Mary Anning

The "Best Collector" award goes to Mary Anning. Anning lived by the sea. She lived in England.

In 1811, her brother found a skull. Anning found the rest of the bones. She was 12 years old at the time. She found a dinosaur. The dinosaur was over 200 million years old. It was the first complete fossil of a dinosaur. Fossils are remains found in rock. Anning was always looking for bones. She found other dinosaurs.

Anning taught herself how to read. She taught herself science. She changed how people thought about Earth's history.

chapter 9

BEST ARTIST

Maria Merian

> In my youth, I spent my time investigating insects.
>
> –Maria Merian

The "Best Artist" award goes to Maria Merian. Merian was born in Germany. She studied nature. She was one of the first to study bugs. She loved bugs as a young child. She collected bugs. She raised silkworms. She kept records.

She was also an artist. She learned to draw and paint. She painted bugs and plants. She started at age 13.

She published her work. She drew pictures. She drew bugs. She drew their life cycles. She drew plants. She was very detailed.

chapter 10

TRENDSETTER

Annie Easley

> I just have my own attitude. I'm out here to get the job done. And I knew I had the ability to do it. And that's where my focus was.
>
> –Annie Easley

The "Trendsetter" award goes to Annie Easley. Easley was a computer scientist. She worked for **NASA**. NASA is in charge of the U.S. space program. Easley was a "human computer." She did math for NASA. She helped send men and rockets to space. She was one of the first to use computers.

When Easley was hired, she was 1 of 4 African Americans. She helped make things fairer. She started wearing pantsuits. Pantsuits are pairs of matching pants and jackets. Easley wore these this instead of wearing dresses or skirts. This was controversial at the time. But Easley did it anyway. She inspired other women in the office to follow. Easley wanted people to focus on what women did. She didn't want the focus to be on what they wore.

chapter 11

BEST FAMILY LEGACY

Mary and Louis Leakey

> I'd rather be in a tent than a house.
>
> –Mary Leakey

The "Best Family Legacy" award goes to Mary and Louis Leakey. The Leakeys were from England. They studied early human beings. They studied prehistory. This is the time of early humans.

The Leakeys met in 1933. Louis was writing a book. He needed someone to draw pictures for him. He hired Mary. The Leakeys fell in love. They got married. They went to East Africa. They dug up places. They found fossils. They worked together for about 30 years. They were a good team.

Once, Louis had the flu. He couldn't dig. But Mary kept working. She found a human fossil that was about 2 million years old!

Mary and Louis had 3 children. One followed in their footsteps.

chapter 12

BEST WRITER

Maria Agnesi

> I hope my studies have brought glory to God ... because that was my father's will. Now I have found better ways and means to serve God, and to be useful to others. –Maria Agnesi

The "Best Writer" award goes to Maria Agnesi. Agnesi was born in 1718. She was born in Italy. She was born into a rich family. At this time, women didn't go to school. Her father encouraged her to learn.

She spoke 7 languages by age 11. She fought for the education of girls. Her education was mostly done with letters. She read books on her own. She wrote to experts to answer her questions. Her father also invited thinkers to the house. These thinkers taught Agnesi. She had a community of experts.

Agnesi wrote a math textbook. She was the first woman to do so. She shaped math education.

Top Memories

- **Around 2700 BCE:** Merit-Ptah served as the chief doctor. Chief means boss. She served in the King's court in ancient Egypt. At this time, many women were doctors. There was even an all-women medical school. Doctors have to know a lot of science.

- **1843:** Ada Lovelace made notes on an important science paper. She described a formula. She's known as the first computer programmer.

- **April 18, 1906:** There was a big earthquake in San Francisco. Alice Eastwood was a botanist. The California Academy of Sciences was burning. Eastwood rescued 1,500 rare plants.

- **1960:** Jane Goodall studied chimpanzees. She did this for over 50 years. She observed that chimpanzees made and used tools.

- **2018:** Dr. Frances Arnold won the Nobel Prize in chemistry. Dr. Donna Strickland won the Nobel Prize in physics. This was the first time that two female scientists won these awards in the same year.

Advice from the Field

Sally Kristen Ride was the first American woman to go into space. She flew on the space shuttle *Challenger*. She did this on June 18, 1983. She used the robotic arm. She was the first woman to do so. She traveled to space a second time. She did this on October 5, 1984. She was first American woman to travel to space twice. She wanted to encourage other girls. She was a role model. She fought for science education. She died in 2012. She was asked how students can prepare to become astronauts. She said, "The most important thing is to start early in middle school or so. You should study math and science. It's not so important to pick one particular area of science. NASA is looking for scientists with backgrounds in all areas. But what is important is to find some area in science or engineering that is very interesting to you, and to pursue it and study it very hard."

Student Life & Clubs

Are you interested in being a scientist? Consider joining Girls Who Code. Girls Who Code is an organization. It wants more women to become computer scientists. It provides different programs. It teaches girls computing skills. It teaches programming. It teaches robotics. It teaches web design. Reshma Saujani founded Girls Who Code. She did this in 2012. She was the first Indian American woman to run for U.S. Congress. She noticed that girls weren't taking computer science classes in schools. She wanted to change this. There are over 1,500 Girls Who Code clubs. The goal is to teach over 1 million girls to code by 2020. Many of the girls pursue STEM jobs. Saujani is proud of the girls. She said, "They are solving problems in their communities, empowering their friends, and defining the future of our world."

"Well-behaved women seldom make history."

–Laurel Thatcher Ulrich

Did You Know...

- There were times when women weren't allowed to go to school. Nuns lived in convents. Convents provided education for many women. That's how many women learned to read and write. Some of these women studied science.
- Chemistry is the study of mixtures. It's the study of how substances change. Ancient Egyptian women may have been the first chemists. They mixed things together. They made perfumes. They made medicine.

Learn More!

Caldwell, S. A. *100 Women Who Made History: Remarkable Women Who Shaped Our World*. New York: DK Publishing, 2017.

Dickmann, Nancy. *Superwomen in STEM: Women Scientists in Life Science*. New York: Gareth Stevens Publishing, 2018.

Ignotofsky, Rachel. *Women in Science: 50 Fearless Pioneers Who Changed the World*. New York: Ten Speed Press, 2016.

Your Turn!

Now, it's your turn! You get to choose the "Top of the Class: Girl Scientist" winner. Who would you pick?

TOP OF THE CLASS: GIRL SCIENTIST

"Top of the Class" means being the best of the best. These prompts will help you think about who'd you pick for the "Top of the Class: Girl Scientist" award:

- Why is this person the best "girl scientist"? List reasons why this person deserves this award more than others.
- Think about how this person is different from girl scientists in this book. What is special about this person?
- How is this person similar to girl scientists in this book? Describe the qualities that girl scientists should have. How does this person represent those qualities?
- How does this person make the world a better place? How does this person change history? Why should we remember this person?
- Girl scientists often struggle. They may also face barriers. They're often told they can't do something. They don't run away when things get hard. How does your person overcome challenges?
- What type of science does this person do? How long has this person been a scientist? What got this person interested in science?
- Many girl scientists spend a lot of time in school. What type of education does this person have? What does this person like to study?

Consider This!

TAKE A POSITION! Gertrude B. Elion won the Nobel Prize in 1988. She said, "I hadn't been aware that there were doors closed to me until I started knocking on them." What does this quote mean? Argue your point with reasons and evidence.

SAY WHAT? There are so many different types of sciences. Examples include physics and biology. What type of science would you like to study? Explain why.

THINK ABOUT IT! Teens spend about 9 hours a day using media. Media includes movies, TV, and internet. Make a list of women you've seen in the media who have STEM roles. How would you increase their presence in the media?

Glossary

astronomy (uh-STRAH-nuh-mee) the science of the study of space

botanist (BAH-tuh-nist) a person who studies plants

comet (KAH-mit) bright object in space with a long tail that travels around the sun

driven (DRIV-en) very determined to succeed

NASA (NAH-suh) National Aeronautics and Space Administration, an organization that is in charge of the U.S. space program

nebulae (NEB-yuh-luh) space clouds of dust and gases

patriotic (pay-tree-AH-tik) being loyal to one's country

physics (FIZ-iks) the science that studies matter and energy

STEM (STEM) science, technology, engineering, and math

vaccine (vak-SEEN) medicine that stops diseases from happening

Index

45th Parallel Press

Published in the United States of America by Cherry Lake Publishing
Ann Arbor, Michigan
www.cherrylakepublishing.com

Reading Adviser: Marla Conn, MS, Ed., Literacy specialist, Read-Ability, Inc.
Book Designer: Jen Wahi

Photo Credits: ©Bain News Service, publisher/Library of Congress/Reproduction No., LC-DIG-ggbain-07682, cover (left), 4; ©NASA, cover (middle), 22; © The History Collection/Alamy Stock Photo, cover (right), 16; ©Science History Images/Alamy Stock Photo, 6; ©Shutter Fairy/Shutterstock, 8; ©Science History Images/Alamy Stock Photo, 10; ©Harris & Ewing/Library of Congress/Reproduction No., LC-USZ62-99090, 12; ©The Picture Art Collection/Alamy Stock Photo, 14; B. J. M. Donne, artist/The Geological Society/GSL/POR/1/Public Domain, 18; Universitätsbibliothek Leipzig/flickr/Public Domain, 20; ©Everett Collection/age footstock, 24; ©Chronicle/Alamy Stock Photo, 26; various art pieces throughout courtesy of Shutterstock

45th Parallel Press is an imprint of Cherry Lake Publishing.

Library of Congress Cataloging-in-Publication Data

Names: Loh-Hagan, Virginia, author.
Title: Girl scientists / by Virginia Loh-Hagan.
Description: Ann Arbor, MI : Cherry Lake Publishing, [2019] | Series: History's yearbook | Audience: Grades 4 to 6. | Includes bibliographical references and index.
Identifiers: LCCN 2019004194| ISBN 9781534147935 (hardcover) | ISBN 9781534150799 (pbk.) | ISBN 9781534149366 (pdf) | ISBN 9781534152229 (hosted ebook)
Subjects: LCSH: Women scientists--Biography--Juvenile literature. | Women in science--History--Juvenile literature. | Science--Biography--Juvenile literature. | Science--History--Juvenile literature.
Classification: LCC Q130 .L64 2019 | DDC 509.2/52--dc23
LC record available at https://lccn.loc.gov/2019004194

Printed in the United States of America
Corporate Graphics

About the Author:

Dr. Virginia Loh-Hagan is an author, university professor, former classroom teacher, and curriculum designer. Her husband is a computer scientist. He does a lot of coding. She lives in San Diego with her very tall husband and very naughty dogs.